Savvy Sayin's

Collected by Ken Alstad

Great Texas Line Press
Fort Worth, Texas

21st Printing

Cover illustration: Mark Hoffer
Cover design: Kari Crane
Page design & layout: Debbie Ford
Woodblocks by Charles Russell & Frederic Remington
Printed by the Swiger family of Hanson Printing, Fort Worth

ISBN: 978-1-892588-42-5

Bulks sales of books from the Great Texas Line are available at special
discounts for fund-raising promotions and other purposes.

Great Texas Line Press
P.O. Box 11105
Fort Worth, Texas 76110
(800) 73TEXAS
greattexas@hotmail.com
www.greattexasline.com

Great Texas Line Press, a socially conscious boutique publishing house launched
during a journalist's mid-life crisis, donates a portion of proceeds from several books
to Habitat for Humanity of Fort Worth, North Fort Worth Historical Society, Texas
Dance Hall Preservation Inc. and Terlingua's Big Bend Educational Foundation. In
addition, hundreds of books are donated annually to public-radio and public-television
stations throughout Texas for their fund-raising efforts.

The future has been losing the wisdom
of the past ever since the freeway
bypassed the corral.

Damn!

FOREWORD

The American language and patterns of speech won't shut up and stand still. People keep stirring them, especially the young, when juices are boiling their blood.

Over the years some changes they made were as giddy as twenty-three-skidoo. Some were linguistically lazy like, you know, man, totally, like, dumb, you know. But not all!

Some have been smart, philosophical or witty. But, if caught in a corner of time, they became quaint, rustic and forgotten. The future lost the wisdom of the past.

Damn!

In Colonial America, Benjamin Franklin was the best-known author of one-liner wit and wisdom. Many sayings in his *Poor Richard's Almanack* are meaningful today; others died or were modified to match new times or places while retaining the basic idea in more modern terms. One such basic idea can serve as an example:

Franklin wrote: *He who hesitates is lost.* Over the years, mothers with daughters changed that to: *She who hesitates is lost.* And today's rush hour drivers prefer: *He who hesitates is rear-ended.*

But a century ago, when that idea came West by Conestoga wagon, Concord stage, or on the rump of a mule, it took on a flavor all its own . . . *The man who straddles the fence gets a sore crotch.*

In territorial days, young men following Horace Greeley's advice sank their spurs in the West and didn't put any hobbles on the language.

Eehaw!

So what if great philosophers proclaimed: *A wise man knows his own ignorance; a fool thinks he knows everything.* Those young men changed that thought to this: *Every jackass thinks he's got horse sense.*

Who cared if folks in the Old States were fond of saying: *One man's meat is another's poison?* Cowpokes made the point more colorfully: *A cowchip is paradise for a fly.*

The Auld Sod was a proper place for this old Irish advice: *There are few wild beats more to be dreaded than a talking man with nothing to say.* But around the corral, this version was it: *The bigger the mouth, the better it looks shut.*

Ain't it a shame we let those sayin's die just because freeways bypassed the corral? They're as useful today as in frontier days. And a lot more interesting than pap on the tongue — in the current, not archaic, meaning of the word.

This, then, is what *Savvy Sayin's* is made of: lean and meaty chunks of Western horse sense with a no-nonsense, colorful candor to match the men and the country.

WHERE THE SAYIN'S CAME FROM

The sayin's in this book are from the author's collection of old-time Western lore and art. The collection was started in 1950 after listening to old-timer survivors of the Territorial days while on assignments as a farm and ranch editor for Arizona newspapers or for magazines covering seven Western states.

Those earlier generations of Americans are now gone, but their spirit lives on in the words they left behind, colorful words that project the personality of the people who said them. Common-sense words rooted in the old-time American principles of independent thinking. Slow-talking words, thoroughly chewed before using. Terse words from people with limited or no formal education, but words with a profundity and insight that today's best thinkers would be hard-pressed to meet or exceed. For example:

What modern health scientist or diet expert could really improve on this old advice: *Too much ain't healthy?* It's a textbook in four words.

Or this 100-year-old sayin': *Lonesome creates diseases that friendship cures?* The insight of this observation can help explain the recent medical discovery that puppies and kittens can work wonders with residents of retirement or nursing homes.

I was thinking of those sayin's in July of 1985 while listening to the radio and browsing through my collection of Western lore. Suddenly, the music was interrupted for a bulletin on President Reagan's progress after his operation, reporting with amazement that he was what Westerners would call "chompin' at the bit to get back to the ranch." Appropriately, a savvy sayin' I had been reading jumped off the page: *A year of nursin' don't equal a day of sweetheart.*

If ever there was a person to whom this sayin' applied first after the assassination try and then after his operation, it certainly was the president. He obviously prefers the sweetheart kind of nursin'.

I marked the sayin' and sent it to Nancy Reagan with the suggestion she show it to the president's doctors. She replied, "I do think more doctors should realize (that this could be) the Real Reason for speedy recoveries . . . more people could probably go home much sooner!"

The letter left me wondering whether other old sayin's could have modern application, one such as this favorite of mine: *Stay shy of a man who's all gurgle n' no guts.*

Now there's advice with real meat to it. Who do you think might say something like that? In these days of slick-tongued spokesmen and packagers of political images, there's only one public person I could think of whose on-the-record statements could match the no-nonsense clarity of that line: the late Barry Goldwater, former senator from Arizona.

I sent the sayin' and a few dozen more selected examples to him, saying I was thinking of putting my collection into book form. He replied, "I think you have one heck of an idea. All of us who were born out here have forgotten the way our fathers and grandfathers spoke, and if we had remembered it, we would all be a lot better off. The Lord knows you understood them when they got it done. Thanks for doing this."

This was getting to be fun — but it was also beginning to sprout a germ of an idea. Some of the old cowboy sayin's sounded vaguely familiar, not because of the actual words used, but in the basic thoughts they expressed. Could they be examples of what happened when the Queen's English was translated into Cowboy Lingo? Some research was called for.

I started thumbing through the books of proverbs and maxims on my shelves. And soon I hit pay dirt in one of my old favorites, one published in London in 1733, back when they still used the funny-looking "s" shaped like an "f" and still capitalized words in the middle of a sentence. The quaint, tongue-boggling title of the book is *Gnomologia: Adagies and Proverbs. Wise and Witty Sayings. Ancient and Modern. Foreign and British.* Certainly anything found in this old book would predate any cowboy's savvy sayin's.

Here's one Olde English example and its savvy sayin' counterpart. O.E.: *The Sussess of Malefactors, authorizes not the crime.* The savvy sayin' counterpart: *A rustler who's never been chased by a posse thinks it's his right to steal.*

Could this old sayin' have been coined by a British settler carrying back-home ideas to the new land? An interesting theory.

Before closing this section, I'd like to share one more example of the timeless quality of these old-time sayin's, this involving a person who shall remain nameless.

She was a cute little slip of a woman. Pert, pretty and in her young 30s. All duded up in her Western clothes, befitting her job as manager of a posh resort motel in Oak Creek Canyon, Ariz.

I showed her one of the sayin's: *Never trust a man who kin look a pretty woman in the eye.*

She blinked, pounded her fist on the counter and said, "Ain't that the truth. Them sonsabitches will look you straight in the eye and tell you anything comes to mind just so's . . ."

I guess those old-time, stove-in cowhands knew what they were talking about. Old truths never die. Some don't even fade away.

A PUBLISHING HOBBY IS BORN

As mentioned earlier, the collection of sayin's was started while I was working as a writer around the West. Even when I got tired of being borderline broke and went Back East for greener pastures, the collection grew from an increasing number of books, magazines and newspapers published during or about the West of the 1800s.

After years of writing jobs around the country, my wife Joann and I retired to Arizona. It lasted six months.

The move had required sorting through the stacks of old books and collections of Western lore and art. And from those stacks and that chore, a new hobby of publishing Old West lore was born. It's our retirement alternative to Arts & Crafts, Spanish as a Second Language and Bring-Your-Own-Water Panning for Gold in a Dry Gulch.

It also is a great way to pay for our summer travel around the West, because we load up to half a ton of publications in the station wagon and hit the road, selling out of the wagon as we go. Which has one slight problem: We don't always make it back to the same dealers each year. Plus one not-so-obvious benefit: We get to see lots more places and meet lots more nice people.

Our dealers tend to be concentrated in areas that fit well with our ideas of retirement travel: near the more spectacular scenic spots, national parks and monuments, theme parks and restored ghost towns. Places like Tombstone, San Francisco, Fish Camp, Las Vegas, Cripple Creek, Santa Fe, Grand Canyon, and, of course, Denver every year. One of our daughters lives there.

On the way we meet a cross-section of people you rarely read about or see on the 10 o'clock news. Wholesome, happy families on vacation from around the world. Mom-and-pop retailers pleased as pups about doing their independent thing. Rodeoers and river raftsmen. Surveyors and salesmen. A storefront lawyer from Haight-Ashbury. Waitresses with baby-fat cheeks and a giggle or sore feet and a smile.

As we ride, we try to outdo each other in spotting unusual businesses: Paradise Apartments & Used Cars, in Missouri. Demolitions & Antiques, near Durango, Colo. Buck's Free Skunk Removal Service, now $5, high up a Rocky Mountain road.

We slow down for deer and armadillo. Wait for a Navajo girl to drive her sheep across the road. Picnic at Grand Canyon with a coyote and jays waiting for handouts. See the sights while calling on concessionaires at tourist attractions. And try to explore different areas each year.

When we get home, there are the few phone calls and letters. Readers who have written or phoned from all the lower 48 states plus Alaska, Canada, England, Sweden, Germany, Holland and Japan . . . people with postmarks not nearly as exciting as the White House or Buckingham Palace or the U.S. Senate, but people with quietly interesting lives.

There's the lady in England who confesses to a bit of a weight problem from a love of strawberries and cream. She sends picture postcards of towns where I was stationed before D-Day. The boy in Oregon who sent some bunkhouse windies he learned from his pioneer grandfather. A man in Illinois who is memorizing the old sayings and getting a reputation as the smartest man in the country. The prospector in Alaska who'd rather be in Arizona come winter and had his general store stock our items for him and his buddies.

The cowhand who needed another copy "cause m'wife cut up the first one to decoupage the bedroom door with the pictures." Wonderful folks, every one.

THE ILLUSTRATIONS

The first illustration in this book is a steel engraving. The rest are woodcuts from the 1800s.

For the uninitiated, woodcuts are made just as the name suggests. The illustrations are cut or carved out of wood. And the carving is done on the end grain of the wood, meaning, if you slice a 2-inch piece out of a tree trunk or branch, the part without the bark is the end grain. It can withstand the hundreds of pounds of pressure of a printing press better than the long-grain section of the wood.

Working from an artist's original drawing or painting, the engraver sketches a mirror-image copy of it on the wood; mirror-imaged because when the woodcut's ink is transferred to paper, the image will be reversed back to the original. Sometimes they goof. (See Remington's signature in the picture at the top of page 53.)

Then, using engraver's chisels called burins, he cuts out all of the white portions of the sketch, leaving raised areas that make the lines of the illustration, lines which are inked for printing.

All but two of the woodcuts in this book are the work of America's two all-time favorite Western artists: Frederic Remington and Charles M. Russell. Both knew the West first-hand during the peak of the cowboy era. They traveled the West with the cowboys and Indians, generals and privates, gamblers and miners, prostitutes and bartenders and sod-busters' wives. They saw first-hand what made the West work, and their work reflected it. The illustrations are from the author's collection.

We hope you will enjoy browsing through these woodcuts and sayin's as much as we did collecting them and seeing them published again.

Ken Alstad
Tucson

Savvy
Sayin's

Some folks got no more conscience than a cow in a stampede.

A guilty man runs when no one's chasin' him.

The good thing about talkin' to your horse is he don't talk back.

A year of nursin' don't equal a day of sweetheart.

A snake-bit man is afraid of a rope.

Sweat is a waste of whiskey.

Kiddin' some folks is like kickin' a loaded polecat.

A cowchip is paradise for a fly.

When you scalp a man more'n once, you begin to run out of hide.

Buckshot means buryin'.

Carnation milk, best in the lan'.
Comes to you in a little red can.
No tits to pull, no hay to pitch.
Jes punch a hole in the sonofa-
bitch.

Silence can be a speech.

Every jackass thinks he's got horse sense.

Frustration is a stump-tailed horse tied short in fly time.

A go-getter is a cowboy who forgot to hobble his horse.

The wildest broncos are those you rode someplace else.

Army mules are branded U.S., meaning unsafe at either end.

If you fall in a cactus patch, you kin expect to pick stickers.

It's easier to stand the smell of liquor than to listen to it.

Brains in the head saves blisters on the feet.

The West is where water has the same value as blood.

If your hoss knew how puny you were, he'd stomp you to death.

There ain't a hoss that cain't be rode. There ain't a man that cain't be throwed.

A man kin easy brag himself out'n a place to lean on the bar.

The cards ain't been shuffled good 'less you got a good hand.

The bobcat sure was planned good. He's got two holes in his hide right were his eyes go.

Never approach a bull from the front, a horse from the rear or a fool from any direction.

Lonesome creates diseases that friendship cures.

A sure cure for a toothache is to tickle a mule's heel.

Too little temptation kin lead to virtue.

Treat mule-headed men the same way you'd treat a mule you're fixin' to corral. Don't try to drive 'em in. Jus' leave the gate open a crack 'n' let 'em bust in.

A hoss thief takes one trail. The posse has to choose from ten.

There's a little boy a'sleepin' in many a grown man you'd call sensible.

A mail-order marriage is trickier'n braidin' a mule's tail.

Never gamble with a man who knows both sides of the cards.

The best way to hold cattle in the winter is to do your slee-pin' in the summer.

Men and barbed wire have their good points.

A lot of a man's religion is in his wife's name.

Lawyers get you out'n the kind of trouble you'd never get in if there was no lawyers.

A loose horse is always lookin' for new pastures.

It's hard to put a foot in a shut mouth.

Surprise is a near-sighted porcupine fallin' in love with a cactus.

Kickin' a man when he's down sometimes is the only way to make him get up.

A man don't have thoughts about women till he's 35. Afore then, all he's got is his feelin's.

Admire a big horse. Saddle a small one.

A man who ain't got ideas of his own should be mighty careful who he borrows 'em from.

A pat on the the back makes some folks' heads swell.

Some fools think they are smart.

Buckshot leaves a mean and oozy corpse.

High-talkin' kin get you leaded.

When a cowboy's too old to set a bad example, he hands out good advice.

Every man is afraid of something.

In a public bath, all men are equal, more or less.

Any rider who brags he ain't been throwed sure ain't forked no bad 'uns.

It's better to say, "Here's where he ran," than, "Here's where he died."

No man in the wrong kin stand up agin' a fellow that's in the right 'n' keeps a'comin.

Stay shy of a man who's all gurgle 'n' no guts.

Some men talk 'cause they got somethin' to say. Others talk 'cause they got to say something.

It's the far-off cows that wear the biggest horns.

The man who uses a "sticky rope" is apt to hang from one.

There are two sides to any man's argument: his and the wrong one.

Jus' 'cause a man ain't yet had a chance to steal don't mean he's honest.

If you're lookin' at the danger end of a scattergun, pull in your horns.

You kin never trust a woman, fleas nor a tenderfoot.

You're in trouble if your neighbor's cows hang around your calf pen and bawl.

Damn-fool mistakes are made by the other guy.

Outlaws and martyrs are greatly improved by death.

Tryin' to get even is a sure sign someone was wrong.

Skill throws more weight than strength.

The best color for a horse is fat.

Any cowboy who says he ain't never been throwed is a liar.

Wild oats make a mighty poor breakfast.

Second-hand gold is as good as new.

Be thankful for fools. Without them, none of us would amount to a damn.

An Old Timer is a man who's had a lot of interesting experiences, some of them true.

A mule is the bastard child of a jackass.

Nerves is just a case of which end of a six-gun you happen to be lookin' at.

You don't need help fallin' down, but a hand up sure is welcome.

If your cows tend more'n one calf at a time, it could be a disease—one that's fatal to you.

Never tire a grass horse.

Having a jealous wife means if you come home with a hair on your coat, you'd better have the horse to match.

You can't tell a horse's gait till she's broke.

Jes' 'cause a trapper is a mite whiffy don't mean he's 'fraid of water. Sometimes he uses it as a chaser.

When you got nothin' to lose, try anythin'.

Easy money is like a shadow. The harder you chase it, the faster it moves.

It's harder to make a banker out of a hoss thief than a hoss thief out of a banker.

Some folks ain't got the brains to be hoss thieves.

Caution should not be too cautious.

A man who was born to drown will drown on a desert.

Nobody but the cattle knows why they stampede, and they ain't talkin'.

An over-polite man is hidin' some mighty unpolite ideas.

It's the switchin' tails that catch the cockleburs.

A cowboy buckin' gamblers don't ride home with his tail up.

Sleepin' late keeps a fellow huntin' his horses.

You kin cut your throat with a sharp tongue.

A corkscrew never pulled no one out of a hole.

Some folks throw too much dust.

Life is one man gettin' hugged for sneakin' a kiss 'n' another gettin' slapped.

A windy is a fellow huntin' grizzlies in camp.

Hoss thieves get hung first 'n' tried later.

Sometimes you'll find a heap of thread on a mighty small spool.

Make good or make tracks.

A cow outfit is no better than its horses.

Hot words lead to cold slabs.

The saloon-keeper loves a drunk, but not as a son-in-law.

The higher you climb, the more rocks you have to dodge.

You can't measure water with a sieve.

Life is like checkers. When you reach the top, you can move wherever you want.

The West is famous for rare and wonderful sights. But the rarest of all is clean socks in a bunkhouse.

No one wants to steal your troubles. No one can steal your good deeds.

Lonesome makes friends of strangers.

Love your enemies but keep your gun oiled.

Man's the only animal who kin get skinned more'n once.

Do not tamper with the natural ignorance of a greenhorn.

It's a sorry cowhand that'll ride a sore-backed hoss.

The man who apologizes when there ain't no need knows something you don't.

Never trust a man who kin look a pretty woman in the eye.

Some men are so well-tempered they can lose it every day and never run out.

If a man who knows you calls you "mister," he don't think too much of you.

Secrets are easy to hear and hard to keep.

It ain't against the law to be comfortable.

The best seasoning for range cooking is a salty sense of humor.

Shallow rivers and shallow minds freeze first.

Don't repent. Stop sinning.

Hoss thieves should be treated like a treasure: buried with care and affection.

A takin' man hates to give.

If someone outdraws you, smile and walk away. There's plenty of time to look tough when you're out of sight.

Some cowboys got too much tumbleweed in their blood to settle down.

The three most fatal diseases in the West are smallpox, cholera and the ignorance to argue with a long-haired, whiskey-drinkin' liar.

A good friend is one who tells you your faults in private.

Before you go into a canyon, know how you'll get out.

Many things are possible if you cinch your attention to them.

Play your hand close to your belly.

You can educate a fool but you can't make him think.

Only a fool spends his life makin' the town smoky.

Some men are so stingy, they'd skin a flea for the hide and tallow.

It's safer to have a good enemy than a bad friend.

Once you start ridin' the high lines, you can't quit no more'n a loser in a poker game.

It's your own fault if you make friends with a hard case.

A man that draws fightin' wages spends a heap of time lookin' for someone to smoke up.

It's easier to catch a horse than break him.

The ignorant hold up trains 'n' stages. The intelligent steal 'em.

Teeth and memory weaken with age.

You can't be hurt by the words you don't say.

A hoss that's fed too much gets ornery.

Hotels in the territory have hot and cold water: hot in the summer and cold in the winter.

Some folks are so soured on life they can't get the acid out'n their systems.

Some towns are so small that when the train pulls into the station, it's out of town.

Some men don't amount to much except around weaklings.

It's better to get it in the neck after a good time than a poor one.

If a cowboy gets bucked off a rabbit-shy horse he gets even. He makes the horse walk back to the ranch all by himself.

When a hen cackles, she's either layin' or lyin'.

Most women are as pretty as kin be.

Small tricks lead to big bullets.

A man who tells you he's no fool has his suspicions.

Pass on good advice. That's all it's good for.

A temper is a valuable thing. Spend it but don't lose it.

Sign in a ranch kitchen:
If you're hungry, grab a plate,
You have my best wishes.
But before you pull freight,
Be sure to wash the dishes.

Tin plates last longer 'cause they're easy to straighten out after a boisterous meal.

Women have more fun because there's more things forbidden to them.

Never trust a man who agrees with you. He's probably wrong.

Some men cain't live without lonesome.

There ain't much paw or bellow to a man who's sure of himself.

If you always do right, you will please some folks and make the rest wonder what you're up to.

The pessimist's problem is he thinks the whole world is just like him.

A good drinking buddy never heard the story before.

Few things are harder to put up with than a good example.

A sharp eye is the mother of good luck.

Fear breeds hate.

Eagles don't catch flies.

Ignorance is expensive.

Sweat never drowned no one.

Married men don't like history too close to home.

You can't tell how good a man or a watermelon is till you thump 'em.

It's fatal to fumble when pullin' your gun.

Drownin' your sorrows only irrigates 'em.

A man who looks for easy work goes to bed tired.

A cat has nine lives, but a lie can live forever.

A heavy saddlebag makes a light heart.

The West is a great playground for young men.

A winning poker hand is like a cowboy's legs: few and far between.

Fear the man who's feared of you.

The man who likes to dabble in gore soon has his appetite for lead soaked up.

A fool kin ask more questions in an hour than 10 savvy men kin ask in a year.

What you cain't duck, welcome.

The fellow who goes around well-heeled sooner or later turns up his toes.

Do not feed nuts to a man with no teeth.

Don't complain of getting old. The only alternative is worse.

You need spurs on a borrowed horse.

If you wake up feelin' halfway 'tween "Oh, Lord," and "My God," you've overdid it.

Suspicion ain't proof.

For some men, it was too late to get wise the day they was born.

Some men never marry 'cause the girls' mothers don't trust 'em too far 'n' the fathers don't trust 'em too near.

Marry a woman with brains enough for two and you'll come out even.

Takin' another man's life don't make no soft pillow at night.

A thief is like a calf. Give him enough rope and he'll tangle hisself.

Shorty didn't know whether to feed or starve his cold, so he drowned it.

It ain't no time to enjoy a smoke when you're a'sittin' on an open keg of powder.

The biggest hosses ain't always the best travelers.

Even a friendly snake is an unwelcome guest.

Age makes a man gentle.

Play 'em high 'n' sleep in the streets.

A man kin learn a heap of things if he keeps his ears washed.

There's no more pleasure in some folks' company than in a wet dog's.

Old age makes you a stranger in your own country.

A good cowman has to know how to lie to the tax collector and cattle buyers.

The man who wears his holster tied down don't do much talkin' with his mouth.

Saddle your horse before sassin' the boss.

The teepee ain't been built that'll hold two families peaceably.

Nothin' gets nothin'.

Some folks can't see no higher than the steam from their own pot of stew.

The wilder the colt, the better the horse.

A man don't get thirsty till he can't get water.

Advice is handy only before trouble comes.

Some men wouldn't know a cactus if they sat on one.

There's nothin' like layin' on your belly 'n' stickin' your muzzle in a clean, runnin' stream.

An honest woman won't take the gift if she don't take the man.

Drownin' is a sure cure for bad habits.

You've got to control yourself before you kin control your horse.

It takes six cups of town coffee to equal one of horseshoe coffee.

Little sins are little sins until a big man commits 'em.

Some men think the sun comes up just to hear them crow.

Very few gunmen are hanged by a legal hangman.

Fore a stable kin get clean, someone has to get dirty.

The man who's always lookin' for trouble hopes he won't find it.

When a woman starts draggin' a loop, there's always some man willin' to step in.

Never straddle a fence. Build one or tear it down.

Calico fever can be fatal for a man's bachelorhood.

A rustler who's never been chased by a posse thinks it's his right to steal.

There's always someone ready to scratch an itchy trigger finger.

When you get up on a mule, keep your eyes on his ears.

When you ain't on speakin' terms with the law, it pays to travel light.

If you ain't got a choice, be brave.

Set your pace by your distance.

A wise cowhand will have something 'sides a slicker for a rainy day.

Happiness depends more on how life strikes you than on what happens.

If you don't buy what you only want, you'll have money to buy what you really need.

A string around the finger helps you remember. A rope around your neck helps you forget.

It's the man who knows how to die standin' up that keeps a'comin'.

Experience is another word for mistakes.

When thieves are around, money is easier to protect than horses. But a fellow with both cain't be too keerful.

A lot of folks would do more prayin' if they could find a soft spot for their knees.

A blind horse kin see just as well from either end.

A politician don't steal elections. He pays for 'em.

The bad wheel creaks the most.

If you have a hill to climb, waitin' won't make it smaller.

A fickle woman and a good-shootin' man are apt to hurt someone.

A pat on the back don't cure saddle galls.

If it ain't broke, don't fix it.

Range cooks are stove-in cowboys too gimpy to work cattle.

A bronc rider should be light in the head and heavy in the seat.

Sign on a wagon:
Pickin' up bones to keep from starvin'
Pickin' up chips to keep from freezin'
Pickin' up courage to keep from leavin'
Way out West in no-man's land.

All some hard cases need is to be scared good 'n' hard 'n' they'll go back to virtuous.

Laugh when you borrow and you'll cry when you pay.

A good horse is never a bad color.

If you have to prove you're right, you're probably wrong.

A drunken tongue tells what's on a sober mind.

What a patent-medicine man tells you, he don't mean. What he means, he don't say.

It don't take long for a gamblin' cowboy to put money in circulation.

Nobody ever died too lazy to take a last breath.

Don't pack hardware for bluff or balance.

Don't count the teeth in someone else's mouth.

Backin' up hard words with gunplay is dangerous business unless you're a top hand at it.

The only place some folks make a name for themselves is on a tombstone.

When there's heroing to be done, someone has to hold the horses.

When a territory gets full of family men and empty of game, it's time to move on or get married.

Borrowin' is like scratchin'. It only feels good for a little while.

Age gentles men and whisky.

There's no room at the chuck wagon for a quitter's blankets.

Wanderin' around like a pony with the bridle off don't get you to the end of the trail.

Broke is what happens when you let your yearnin's get ahead of your earnin's.

Some men get callouses from pattin' themselves on the back

If the wife of a patent-medicine man kisses you, count your teeth.

If you think you've forgotten something, you have.

You can't get to the end of a trail by wanderin' like a pony who's slipped his bridle.

A bronc rider should be light in the head and heavy in the seat.

When two play, one wins.

There ain't no way to practice gettin' hung.

If you follow a new track, there ain't no way of knowin' if the man that made it knew where he was goin'.

A man who confesses to small faults hopes you will think he has no big ones.

Never spur a horse when he's swimmin'.

It's less painful to be dead drunk than dead hungry.

A man's eyes tell you what his mouth is a'feared to say.

Some folks are pleased to have a feather in their cap. Others want the whole war bonnet.

Don't trust a wolf for dead till he's been skun.

Out West, every prairie dog hole is a gold mine, every hill is a mountain, every creek is a river and every prospector is a liar.

When a hypochondriac has measles, he tells you how many.

Murderers and horse thieves are often found in a state of suspense.

A prospector is a cowboy with his brains knocked out.

A six-gun might cripple you, but buckshot means buryin'.

Never draw a gun unless you mean to shoot.

The food on some ranches might be a mite weak-tastin', but the coffee's strong enough to bring up the average.

Don't build the gate till you've built the corral.

You can't beat experience for sweatin' the fat off'n the brain.

With the homestead law, the U.S. is betting you 140 acres that you can't live on it.

If the coffee tastes like mud, remember it was ground this morning.

For better or for worse means for good.

The man who can't take a word of criticism hears it the most.

It's mighty hard to do what your neighbors ain't.

Assets are baby donkeys.

Every man has equal liberty to seek his own level.

Whiskey makes a man see double and feel single.

A brave man doesn't admit courage. Cowards don't admit fear.

If someone would pump some water into it, an arroyo would be a river.

Pullin' a loaded rifle barrel first out of a wagon is like ridin' a mule's tail. Both kin get your gut shot.

Take care of yourself as well as you do your horse and you'll both be healthy.

Lightning does the work; thunder takes the credit.

Range horses are dangerous at both ends.

Skin your own deer.

A smile from a good woman is worth more'n a dozen handed out by a bartender.

Never do wrong when people are watchin'.

It's a sure sign of bad luck to bet on the wrong horse.

Drunks sober up. Fools remain fools.

Any cowboy kin carry a tune. The trouble comes when he tries to unload it.

Why is it when it rains good things, we've left our slickers at the wagon?

Two names are too heavy to carry if you're travelin' fast.

Pullin' up the town to look at its roots don't help it grow more.

Some men got more guts than gumption.

You don't get splinters from wrestling timber wolves.

A wink is as good as a nod to a blind mule.

Spread happiness where you go, not when.

A heap depends on the breed and age of a dog whether he'll bite the hand that feeds him.

You cain't tell how fast a jackrabbit will run by the length of his ears.

Many a thing a man does is judged right or wrong according to the time and place.

Hanging is a legal death trap.

You kin wash your hands but not your conscience.

Even the biggest ball of twine unravels.

The stuff that makes you tipsy makes you tip your hand.

Secrets are easier heard than kept.

You can't tell how far a frog will jump or a horse will run by the color of his hide.

The business end of a six-gun don't pay no interest.

You can't head off a man who won't quit.

Run when you're wrong, shoot when you're right.

You kin talk sense to a smart man but not a fool.

Tryin' to run a brand with a cold iron don't save no time.

Some folks speak the God's truth only when they admit to lyin'.

Roller towels suffer from being a mite too popular.

An optimist is a man who, when she says, "I'm tellin' you no for the last time," he says, "I knew you'd weaken in time."

Some men's wives are angels. The others are still alive.

The really great man makes everyone else feel great.

One sure way to land in Boot Hill is to shoot without aiming.

Morning-after questions: How many men did I whip? Did anyone get killed? Is there something wrong with my eyes? Whose boots am I wearing?

If you toss a rope five times and miss, the only thing left to do is lie.

Most gunmen wiggle their trigger fingers once too often.

If she says, "No," you haven't asked the right question or the question right.

When things don't please you, the best medicine is to swallow a little tincture of time.

Don't point a gun at nobody you ain't willin' to shoot if necessary.

Priceless ain't free.

Strangers are more so east of the Missouri.

A stone stops rollin' when it finds the kind of moss it wants to gather.

If you've lived to be 29 and have made no enemies, you're a failure.

When in doubt, let your horse do the thinkin'.

Tex has been crippled up with all the old cattleman's ailments ever since he discovered redeye was a good painkiller for all the old cattleman's ailments.

Tossin' a rope before buildin' a loop don't catch the calf.

Important comes in two sizes: yours and mine.

Hate is like water in a dry gulch. The longer it runs, the deeper it digs.

A wishbone ain't no substitute for a backbone.

A cowboy is a hired hand on horseback.

A good friend is a man who rolls his own hoop.

Some folks have their good points, but they keep jabbin' you with 'em like they were spurs.

Every town has a couple with the same likes and dislikes: They like to fight, and they hate each other.

The town drunk has a lot of horse sense. You can lead him to water but he won't drink it.

A confirmed liar is a man who, even when he admits he's lying, no one believes.

It kin be unlucky to postpone a marriage — once.

Never marry a woman with the kind of looks you'd like to see on another man's wife.

The only kind of equality that counts is being equal to the occasion.

A gentle horse is soon curried.

Cowboys don't play poker for money. Dealers do.

You can't drive a range-raised horse over a rattlesnake.

Many things should be done in silence, and talkin' about them is a mistake.

The rider of a rough string may be short on brains but not guts.

A high-talkin' man kin quick brag hisself into buryin' or buzzard bait.

Some men never reach a marriageable age.

A man' kin die from a good poker hand — if it's too good, like five aces.

On a roundup, it's OK to eat with your fingers. The food is clean.

Arizona is no place for amateurs.

A dead man's shroud has no pockets.

Most folks are just about as happy as they've made up their minds to be.

Most gossip ain't worth the repeatin' it gets.

A six-inch rain in Arizona is one drop every six inches.

Careful is a naked man climbin' a bobwire fence.

Thieves are presumed innocent till proved guilty, but a man with a starched collar has to prove himself.

The man who can't make a choice makes a choice.

Men honor men who honor their fellow man.

When you hear night birds call in the daytime and follow you along the trail, it's time to head for cover.

On a gentle horse, every man is a rider.

There's always a few longhairs who do their damnedest to fertilize the cow.

Some men are like the sky. The only time they're quiet is when they're blue.

A bronco has to have his spree when the humor strikes him; afterwards he'll behave for months.

He thought she was his'n. He learned he was her'n.

A loud mouth and a shallow brain go well together.

Hard-boiled eggs tend to be yellow inside.

A self-made man worships his creator.

To avoid temptation, yield.

It's all right to take your time in a gunfight just as long as you're the first to shoot.

The man who knows the least repeats it the most.

A puny man can't afford to get mad.

The ranch that has real milk, butter and eggs is an oasis in the territory's bill of fare.

Poor is having to sell the horse to buy the saddle.

An Injun haircut calls for a certain amount of hide.

Foreman: "I'm a man of few words. If I say come, you come." Cowboy: "I'm a man of few words, too. If I shake my head, I ain't comin'."

Weigh words, don't count 'em.

Time is the best doctor.

To learn what money is worth, try to borrow some.

Always ride on the high side when there's folks around that ain't declared their intentions.

A man is as good as his nerves.

Bein' too positive in your opinions kin get you invited to a dance — in the street, to the music of shots, nicely aimed.

Shorty never learned to spell 'cause the teacher kept changin' the words.

Even a blind pig will find an acorn once in a while.

When the law pins a star on a man's brisket, it don't make him no wiser. But if he don't abuse it, it gives his wisdom power for right.

A chip on the shoulder is a sure sign of a blockhead.

Some folks follow old wagon tracks. Others break new trails.

If it takes liquor to build your courage, you might have to prove it.

Stick your nose in trouble and you're likely to find your foot's in there, too.

Food for thought gives some folks indigestion.

The least said, the soonest mended.

Cowboys are paid $30 a month to outthink cows.

The population of some small towns never changes. Every time a baby is born, someone leaves town.

A man who hunts trouble in a saloon is apt to pass in his chips with sawdust in his beard.

A man that packs his gun loose don't run his heels over sidesteppin' trouble.

Don't interfere with nothin' that don't bother you.

Sometimes it's safer to pull freight than your gun.

It's the little things that get tangled in your spurs that trip you up.

It takes a range-reared hoss to work cattle — one that kin rustle 'n' live on grass.

A toothless dog chews careful.

The farther you run, the longer the way back.

By the rules of gunfighting, the loser is wrong.

Broke is ordering oyster stew 'n' hopin' to find a pearl so's you kin pay for the meal.

Some folks look at their own common sense through a magnifying glass.

Don't try to stop a fight till it's over.

A man that's quick of tongue might have to be quick on the trigger.

When a man calls your bluff, it's time to look at your hole card again.

Don't laugh at another hombre's trouble.

The West is a good country for men and dogs but mighty hard on women and oxen.

Some friends are friends only up to the pockets.

It's the man that's the cowboy, not the outfit he wears.

A tombstone can stand upright and lie on its face at the same time.

Some folks change their minds as easy as an Injun changes camp.

Life ain't in holdin' a good hand but in playin' a poor one well.

Never try to drown your sorrows if she kin swim.

Don't fork a saddle if you're scared of gettin' throwed.

The West don't care what a man calls himself. It's what he calls others that lets him stay healthy or not.

A man loses his dreams, his teeth and his follies in that order.

It's the absent who are judged guilty.

A politician can borrow $20, pay back $10 and declare you're even 'cause you both lost $10.

Approach a mule the way a porcupine makes love: slow 'n' keerful.

If you want to leave your mark, don't let the sun catch you in bed.

Polishin' your boots on a brass rail is dangerous to your wealth.

A full house divided wins no pot.

A man who keeps his eyes on the horizon like he's expectin' the sheriff to budge up on him has more on his mind than seein' the sights.

On the range, a man's home is apt to be his saddle blanket 'n' the first thing you know, he's moved it to Texas.

If you'd like to know a man, find out what makes him mad.

Many a man would rather leave his hide on a fence than stay in a corral.

You never know your luck till the wheel stops.

You'll never find a hired gun sittin' on his gun hand.

You're bound to succeed if you have ignorance and confidence.

Circuit-ridin' preachers are so poor that if they didn't fast twice a week, they'd starve to death.

You'll sure get out-pointed if you pick a fight with a porcupine.

There ain't many tears shed at a Boot Hill buryin'.

Never pack a six-gun with six pills in the wheel. If you cain't do the job with five shots, it's time to get the hell out of there.

When you beat a man at his own game, you've had all the revenge you need--unless you're a hog.

Anyone kin look tall when surrounded by shorties.

Next to hoss rustlin', curiosity is the most dangerous crime.

Stealin' for charity is stealin'.

Nerve succeeds.

Do not desire what you can't acquire.

It's better to know the country than to be the best cowboy.

It's easy to fill the shoes of a big-headed man.

The best way to convince a tenderfoot is to let him have his own way.

Ugly women hate mirrors.

A faint heart never filled a flush.

The jealous man soon learns to hate.

If you see a coward with a gun, it's time to get scared or scarce.

The man who keeps a bridle on his temper shoots the truest.

Be mighty careful in your choice of enemies.

Close friends are folks who've sopped gravy out'n the same skillet.

Folks that always ride in a high lope miss the fun along the trail.

A change of pasture kin make the calf fatter.

You cain't never tell which way a pickle will squirt.

No matter how hard the winter, spring always comes.

When the boss wants a long talk, you're in for a long listen.

Don't leave a traveled road to follow a trail.

Young liars turn into old thieves.

The hottest fire is made by the wood you chop yourself.

After some folks tell you all they know, they keep on talkin'.

Worry is like a rockin' horse. It's something to do that don't get you nowhere.

Immigrants coming west to look for gold were born silly and had a relapse.

There's always someone to take the slack out of a trouble-maker's rope.

You can't hurt a tongue by speakin' softly.

If you must be a fool, be a rich fool 'n' people will treat you like a king.

A crooked tree will never straighten its branches.

Some folks' morals are as loose as a busted egg.

Money is like a drunk. The tighter it gets, the louder it talks.

When wiser men are talkin', let your ears hang down and listen.

Adios.

More wit and wisdom from Great Texas Line Press

You Know You're a Texan If...
Texas author and humorist Mike Nichols expounds on just
the wackiest things that make one a true son or daughter of
this singular State of Mind. "More laughs per square inch
than any book I've read." —*Abilene Reporter-News*
80 pages. Paperback. ISBN 978-1-892588-31-9

Speak Texan in 30 Minutes or Less
A humorous guide to understanding why Texans speak the way
they do. "Explains the meaning of Texan-speak" —*San Angelo
Standard-Times*
80 pages. Paperback. ISBN 978-1-892588-10-4

Texas Speak Advanced Course
This dog will hunt! An absolutely humorous guide to deci-
phering Lone Star lingo. "A funny book that strikes a truthful
note." —*Amazon.com* review.
80 pages. Paperback. ISBN 978-1-892588-15-9

100 Great Things About Texas
A celebration of 100 subtle, and not so subtle, serious and not
so serious, things that make Texas the special place that it is.
"This is one of those little stocking-stuffer books that's simply
a fun read." —*Bryan-College Station Eagle*
104 pages. Paperback. ISBN 978-1-892588-29-6

Texas Redneck Road Trips
Ever hanker to swim with gators, snare huge catfish by hand,
shoot feral hogs from a helicopter or just sit throw back a free
Shiner Bock? Learn how to in this "mini guide to some of the
Lone Star State's unique and intriguing attractions." —*Fort
Worth Star-Telegram*
120 pages. Paperback. ISBN 978-1-892588-36-4